Revolting Reptiles

Lynn Huggins-Cooper

QEB Publishing

Published in the United States by
QEB Publishing, Inc.
3 Wrigley, Suite A
Irvine, CA 92618

www.qeb-publishing.com

Library of Congress Cataloging-in-Publication Data

Huggins-Cooper, Lynn.
  Revolting reptiles / Lynn Huggins-Cooper.
     p. cm. -- (Awesome animals)
  Includes index.
  ISBN 978-1-59566-564-5
  1. Reptiles--Juvenile literature. 2. Reptiles--Behavior--
Juvenile literature. I. Title.
  QL644.2.H847 2009
  597.9--dc22

                                        2008011768

Author: Lynn Huggins-Cooper
Edited, designed, and picture researched
by:
  Starry Dog Books Ltd.
Consultant: Sally Morgan

Publisher: Steve Evans
Creative Director: Zeta Davies
Senior Editor: Amanda Askew

Printed and bound in the United States of America in North
Mankato, Minnesota

092809
QED 10-2009 4

Picture credits
Key: t = top, b = bottom, l = left, r = right, c = center,
FC = front cover, BC = back cover.

A = Alamy, C = Corbis, D = Dreamstime.com, G = Getty Images,
ISP = iStockphoto.com, PL = Photolibrary, PS = Photoshot,
S = Shutterstock.com, SDB = Starry Dog Books, SPL = Science
Photo Library.

1 C/ © Joe McDonald; 2–3 S/ © Alex James Bramwell; 3br
S/ © Snowleopard1; 4t ISP/ © Klaus Nilkens, 4b S/ © Dr
Morley Read; 5 S/ © Snowleopard1; 6t G/ © Claus Meyer, 6b
Wikipedia; 7 G/ © Pete Oxford; 8t S/ © Olga Bogatyrenko,
8b C/ © Arthur Morris; 9 A/ © Juniors Bildarchiv; 10t PS/ ©
Jean-Louis Le Moigne/NHPA, 10b C/ © Michael & Patricia
Fogden; 11 ISP/ © Kris Hanke; 12 C/ © Joe McDonald;
13t ISP/ © Bob Kupbens, 13b G/ © Mark Moffett; 14b S/ ©
Snowleopard1, 14–15 C/ © Wolfgang Thieme/dpa; 15b SPL/
© Paul Zahl; 16t C/ © Joe McDonald, 16b C/ © Theo Allofs;
17 ISP/ © Norman Bateman; 18t G/ Pete Oxford, 18b PL/
© Joe McDonald; 19 G/ © Mike Severns; 20t C/ © Michael
& Patricia Fogden, 20b ISP/ © Tillsonburg; 21 C/ © Theo
Allofs/zefa; 22–23b C/ © Frans Lanting; 23t ISP/ © Timothy
Martin, 23b PS/ © Daniel Heuclin/NHPA; 24t PS/ © Kevin
Schafer/NHPA, 24b PL/ © Zigmund Leszczynski; 25 A/ ©
Mark Bowler Amazon-Images; 26bl PS/ © Ken Griffiths/
NHPA, 26–27 S/ © John Bell; 27b C/ © Lynda Richardson; 28
(all photos) SDB/ © Nick Leggett; 29 SDB/ © Nick Leggett.

Contents

Cold blood!

Reptiles include lizards, snakes, and crocodiles. **Amphibians** include soft-skinned frogs and salamanders. Both amphibians and reptiles are cold-blooded animals, which means that their body temperature is the same as the temperature of the surrounding air.

▲ *Like modern crocodiles, the* **dinosaur T-rex** *had sharp teeth for grabbing food.*

Reptiles old and new

Dinosaurs were reptiles that lived millions of years ago. Like modern reptiles, they had no fur and they hatched from eggs. The teeth and skin of some dinosaurs were similar to those of modern alligators, and some dinosaurs may have been as intelligent as crocodiles. Dinosaurs are now **extinct**.

◀ *Many salamanders, such as the Ecuador mushroomtongue salamander, do not have lungs or* **gills**. *They get the oxygen they need through their skin.*

4

Amphibians

Amphibians have **adapted** to life in and out of water. They are able to breathe through their skin, although most adult amphibians also have lungs for breathing. When they face a **predator**, many amphibians pretend to be dead, in the hope that the predator will leave them alone. Some amphibians produce **toxins** in their skin that make them taste bad to predators.

◀ *Poison-dart frogs have poisonous skin. Local tribespeople in South America rub the frogs against the skin of young parrots. The poison makes the parrots grow feathers of different colors.*

Funky frogs

Frogs live all over the world, except in icy **Antarctica**. Most **species** live in **tropical** countries with warm, damp climates, but some prefer hot deserts. Some frogs have developed unusual ways of protecting their young.

▼ *This frog is not shown life-sized here. At only 1 inch (25 millimeters) long, the pouched frog is about the size of a cherry.*

▲ *The paradox frog makes a grunting noise like a pig. It digs in the muddy bottoms of ponds to find insects and* ***larvae*** *to eat.*

Paradox frog

The paradox frog lives in ponds and lakes in South America and on the Caribbean island of Trinidad. Adult paradox frogs are about 2 inches (6 centimeters) long, but their **tadpoles** are much larger, at up to 9 inches (22 centimeters) long. As the tadpoles develop into adults, they shrink.

Pouched frog

The pouched frog lives in a small area of central-eastern Australia. Unusually, the female lays a pile of eggs in damp soil rather than in water. As the eggs hatch into tiny, white tadpoles, the male hops into the middle of the pile, and the tadpoles wriggle into two pouches just above his back legs. The tadpoles stay in his pouches until they are ready to emerge as fully formed, small frogs.

Lake Titicaca frog

The Lake Titicaca frog lives only in Lake Titicaca in South America. Lake Titicaca is 12,500 feet (3812 meters) above sea level. At this **altitude**, the air is very thin—it has less oxygen than places nearer sea level. To cope with this, the Lake Titicaca frog has developed saggy skin with many folds. The frog soaks up oxygen through its skin and the extra skin increases the amount of oxygen that it can absorb.

▼ *The Lake Titicaca frog can survive underwater as it absorbs oxygen from the water through its skin. It sometimes does strange "press-ups" underwater that disturb the water and make more oxygen flow.*

Beastly biters

Alligators, crocodiles, and the Indian gharial have lots of terrifying teeth. They grow replacements if their teeth are lost or broken.

Alligators

There are two species of alligator—the huge American alligator and the much smaller Chinese alligator, which is almost extinct. Alligators live in swamps, freshwater ponds, rivers, and **wetlands**. They pounce on their prey, which include reptiles, **mammals**, and birds, if they get too close.

▼ *An alligator kills its prey, such as this brown pelican, by gripping it and pulling it underwater until it drowns.*

▲ *The male gharial has a small growth on the end of its snout. It uses this to make a humming noise that warns off other males, and to blow bubbles that attract females.*

Indian gharial

The Indian gharial lives in small numbers in the rivers of north-east India, Bangladesh, Nepal, and Bhutan. Large males can reach almost 20 feet (6 meters) long. The gharial is clumsy on land, but very quick in the water. It catches small fish and other creatures by snapping its jaws as it sweeps its head from side to side.

Caimans

Caimans are the largest predators in South America's **Amazon basin**. They can reach 13 to 16 feet (4 to 5 meters) long—the length of an average estate car. Caimans eat fish, including piranhas, which are aggressive meat eaters themselves. They also eat turtles, birds, deer, **tapirs**, and even **anacondas**.

▼ *An adult caiman swallows a large fish whole. The acid in the caiman's stomach is so strong that it can digest every part of its prey, including bones and tough skin.*

Foul fact!

During the dry season, caimans crowding together in small ponds have been known to eat each other.

Nasty noises

Some reptiles and amphibians make creepy noises, which can be very loud. Some let out strange screams. Others imitate the noises made by other animals.

▼ *This smoky frog is swallowing a masked puddle frog whole. As well as other frogs, the smoky frog will eat small birds, mammals, and even snakes that are twice its own size.*

▲ *A male midwife toad will carry eggs on its back legs until they hatch.*

Midwife toads

Midwife toads live in northern Africa and parts of Europe. The males make a noise that sounds like an electronic bleep. The females lay strings of eggs, which the males stick to their legs using slime. When the eggs are ready to hatch into tadpoles, the males wade into the water so the tadpoles can swim off.

Smoky frog

The smoky frog, or smoky jungle frog, lives mainly in tropical rain forests in Central and South America. If attacked, the smoky frog makes a high-pitched scream.

▼ *Unlike many frogs, coqui frogs do not have webbed feet. They have discs or pads on their toes that help them to grip onto plants.*

Coqui frogs

The name of these frogs is pronounced co-KEE, which sounds like the noise they make. Coqui frogs originally lived on several Caribbean islands, but they are also found in huge numbers on the islands of Hawaii. They reached Hawaii by accidently hopping aboard cargo ships.

Foul fact!

Coqui frogs make a noise that measures 90 to 100 decibels 1.5 feet from the frog. This is as loud as a speeding express train.

Poisonous pests

Some reptiles and amphibians are very poisonous. They might have poison in their skin, their **saliva**, or their **venomous** fangs.

▼ *The horned viper has two long scales on its head that look like horns. The horns may help to protect the snake's eyes, and may also make the snake harder for predators to spot.*

Horned viper

The horned viper lives in northern Africa and parts of the Middle East. When hunting, it digs its body into the sand and lies in wait. The only parts of the snake that remain visible are its horns. When prey approaches it suddenly lurches out of the sand and strikes, shooting poison from its fangs. The horned viper preys on unwary **rodents**, such as rats, as well as small snakes, lizards, and birds.

A drug made from the saliva of the Gila monster is being used in the United States to treat diabetes.

▲ *The Gila monster has powerful claws for digging burrows but kills with poisonous saliva.*

Gila monster

The Gila monster is a lizard. It kills and eats birds, rodents, and other lizards by biting them and then chewing until venomous saliva flows into the wound. The Gila monster lives in the south-west of the United States and in northern Mexico. Its teeth are loose and if a few get broken, it just grows some more.

Poison-dart frogs

Poison-dart frogs are found in Central and South America and most are brightly colored to warn predators that they are dangerous to eat. They **secrete**, or release, poison through their skin.

▶ *The most toxic poison-dart frog is the golden poison frog, which carries enough poison to kill up to ten humans.*

Sneaky salamanders

Many salamander species are known for having a sneaky trick. If a predator grabs the salamander by the tail, part of the tail breaks off and wriggles about like a separate creature. This distracts the predator so the salamander can run away unharmed.

▼ *Mole salamanders have smooth, shiny skin that can absorb oxygen.*

Fire salamander

The fire salamander lives in the forests of southern and central Europe. It hunts mainly at dusk and during the night for insects, spiders, slugs, worms, and other small creatures, such as newts and young frogs. When it is not hunting, it hides under stones and logs.

Mole salamanders

Mole salamanders live in North America, in woodland and grassland areas. They live in burrows that they have dug, or in holes that have been abandoned by other small creatures. Some mole salamanders spend all winter in their burrows, but return to the ponds where they were born when it is time to breed.

▼ *If threatened, the fire salamander sprays a poisonous, milky fluid from glands along its back at the predator.*

Hellbenders

Hellbenders, or giant salamanders, live in Japan, China, and North America. The two North American species grow up to 16 inches (40 centimeters) long, but their Japanese cousin grows up to 6 feet (1.8 meters) long. Hellbenders eat virtually any living thing that they find in the water, including **crayfish**, worms, and insects.

▶ *Hellbenders have wrinkly skin that oozes slime. The slime protects them from cuts and attacks from parasites.*

Foul fact!

In North America, hellbenders have many names including devil dog and snot otter!

Beware dragons!

Some reptiles look like dragons and are even called dragons. They have scaly skin, long claws, and some have spikes all down their back.

Komodo dragon

The Komodo dragon of Indonesia grows up to 10 feet (3 meters) long and is the largest species of lizard. It has a big appetite and can eat up to 80 per cent of its body weight in one meal. It eats other reptiles, birds, monkeys, goats, deer, horses, and water buffaloes.

▲ *Like many lizards, the Chinese water dragon can sense light through a small bump on the top of its head called a "**third eye**."*

Chinese water dragon

The Chinese water dragon lives in the rain forests of South East Asia. It often sits on branches overhanging water, and if startled, drops into the water and swims away. It can stay underwater for up to 30 minutes. The Chinese water dragon eats insects, small fish, rodents, and plants.

◀ *The Komodo dragon has long claws for catching hold of prey. It bites off chunks of meat with its teeth. Its saliva is filled with bacteria that help to kill its prey quickly.*

Some people eat green iguanas. The dish is known as "bamboo chicken."

Green iguana

The green iguana looks like a wingless dragon. It grows up to 6.5 feet (2 meters) long and has pointed scales along its back. Although it looks fierce, the green iguana is a herbivore, which means it eats only plants. It lives in Central and South America.

▲ The green iguana's long fingers and claws enable it to climb trees and cling onto branches.

Bizarre creatures

Reptiles and amphibians have some amazing habits. One lizard, the common basilisk, can actually run across water.

Common basilisk

A young common basilisk can run about 33 to 66 feet (10 to 20 meters) across the surface of water without sinking. It does this when fleeing from predators. The common basilisk lives near streams and lakes in the rain forests of Central and South America. It eats insects, flowers, and small creatures, such as fish, snakes, and birds.

▶ *Webbing between the toes of the common basilisk helps it to run across water. On land, the webbing is rolled up.*

▲ *Common rain frogs get their name from their habit of calling during rainstorms.*

Common rain frogs

Tiny common rain frogs live in the rain forests of Central and South America, on some Caribbean islands, and in southern Africa. They lay their eggs in a cup of leaves or on a moist patch of the forest floor. The eggs hatch into frogs rather than tadpoles.

Foul fact!

According to legend, the basilisk could kill things just by looking at them.

Jackson's chameleon

The Jackson's chameleon comes from eastern Africa and has been introduced in Hawaii. The babies are born fully developed, rather than hatching from eggs.

◀ *The Jackson's chameleon is able to look in two directions at once. Males have three long horns.*

Peculiar predators

Some reptiles and amphibians use a **lure** to attract prey. Others wait silently in hiding until prey passes and then launch a sudden attack.

Alligator snapping turtle

The alligator snapping turtle lives in North America. It has a small, wormlike growth on its tongue that it wriggles to attract prey, especially fish. It also eats frogs, small snakes, birds, and small animals.

▲ *The death adder has a thick body and a short tail. It takes 2 to 3 years to reach adult size.*

Death adders

Death adders live in Australia and New Guinea. They bury themselves in sand or **leaf litter**, so that only the head and tail are visible. To attract prey, the death adder dangles the tip of its tail, which looks like a worm. When a bird or mammal tries to grab the "worm," the death adder strikes and poisons its prey in a fraction of a second.

◀ *The alligator snapping turtle's jaws are strong enough to bite off a human finger.*

Surinam horned frog

The Surinam horned frog lives in northern South America. It burrows itself into the ground and waits for prey. If a mouse, small lizard, or frog wanders past, the Surinam horned frog jumps out and grabs it.

▼ *The Surinam horned frog is well camouflaged. The pattern on its skin makes it looks like a leaf, so that it is difficult to see on the forest floor.*

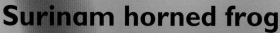

Foul fact!

Some Surinam horned frog tadpoles will eat each other after they hatch.

Tricky tongues

The tongues of some reptiles are extremely long and sticky. Some have tongues that are V-shaped, and some have brightly colored tongues that they stick out to scare away predators.

▼ *With incredible speed, a Parson's chameleon shoots its tongue out at an insect on a twig. It can capture prey up to one-and-a-half body lengths away.*

Chameleons

When a chameleon sees prey, such as a grasshopper, cricket, or praying mantis, it aims its long, sticky tongue at the animal. As the tip of the chameleon's tongue hits the prey, it forms a cup shape that sticks to the creature and traps it. The chameleon then pulls the insect back into its mouth. Some large chameleons also eat other lizards and small birds.

Diamondback rattlesnakes

The two species of diamondback rattlesnake are North America's most poisonous snakes. They are aggressive, but warn predators of their presence by shaking the rattle at the end of their tail.

▲ *The diamondback rattlesnake has a large, forked tongue which can "taste" the scent of prey on the air.*

Blue-tongued skinks

Blue-tongued skinks live in Australia and New Guinea. They sleep in leaf litter or fallen logs, and during the day hunt for snails, slugs, insects, spiders, berries, flowers, **fungi**, and **carrion**. Although their teeth are not sharp, they can give a powerful bite.

▶ *When alarmed, the blue-tongued skink sticks out its blue tongue to scare away predators.*

Terrifying toads

Toads tend to travel further from water than frogs, and their skin is often dry and bumpy, rather than smooth.

▲ *The female star-fingered toad carries her eggs buried in the skin of her back.*

African clawed toad

The African clawed toad lives in water. It uses its claws to stir up mud to find insects to eat. If the toad's pond dries up, it buries itself in the mud and waits until it rains.

Star-fingered toads

Star-fingered toads, also called Surinam toads, live in the Amazon region of South America. When the female lays her eggs, they stick to her back with slime and gradually sink into her skin. About 12 to 20 weeks later, the babies push their way out of her skin and swim off.

◀ *The African clawed toad uses its sensitive fingers to find and catch prey. It uses its back feet to dig down into mud.*

Giant cane toad

The giant cane toad is from Central and South America. In 1935, it was introduced to Australia to control a beetle that was damaging sugar cane crops. The toad bred quickly, and is now a pest itself. Pets, humans, and the **native** animals that prey on frogs and toads all fall victim to its poison.

▼ *The giant cane toad produces a poison from glands on each shoulder. If humans eat the poison, it can cause them to have a heart attack.*

Foul fact!

The largest giant cane toad was 9 inches (23 centimeters) long—the size of a small dog!

Amazing adaptors

To help them to survive, some reptiles and amphibians have changed, or adapted, over time to new conditions. In hot, dry places they may live mainly underground away from the heat of the sun, and only come out when it rains.

Water storing frog

The water storing frog lives in Australia. The frog stores water in large quantities in its **bladder** for use in dry periods. In hot conditions, it burrows into the mud and makes an underground hole, or cell. It may sleep there for several years, waiting for cooler, wetter weather to arrive.

Tokay

The tokay is a **gecko**. It has developed special clingy toe pads for gripping. The pads are covered in tiny hairs. The ends of these hairs are split into many parts. These tiny hairs can stick to smooth surfaces. To release its grip, the tokay curls its toes. It lives in South East Asia, north-east India, Bangladesh, and New Guinea.

◀ *The water storing frog is only seen after heavy rain. When the male calls, it inflates its throat to make the sound louder.*

▲ *The tokay's soft, velvety skin is colored to help it blend in with tree bark.*

Sirens

Sirens live in the southern United States, in shallow pools and ditches that dry up in warm weather. When their pools dry up, sirens burrow into the mud and make a **cocoon** out of hardened slime and old skin. Large adults can survive in this way, without food, for nearly two years.

▶ *Sirens have a horny, beaklike mouth and a pair of tiny front legs, but no back legs.*

Make it!

Make your own poisonous pet. Use card and fabric to make a scary snake.

✂ **You will need:**

Craft paper or thin card
Scissors
Sticky tape
Newspaper
Large piece of fabric
Glue
Rubber band
Glitter
Ribbon

3 Cut a strip of fabric 7x23.5 inches (17x60 centimeters) long. Glue the hollow segment next to one short edge of the fabric. Then add the other segments in a row, leaving slight gaps between them.

4 Cut out a 12-inch (30-centimeter) square of fabric. Scrunch up some newspaper into a ball. Wrap the fabric around the ball and attach with a rubber band.

1 From a sheet of craft paper, cut a strip 6x16 inches (14x40 centimeters). Roll it into a long tube and secure with sticky tape.

2 Cut the tube into five equal segments. Stuff four of them with newspaper so they keep their shape.

5 Stuff the ends of the fabric into the hollow segment and use sticky tape to fix it to the inside of the tube. Wrap the long piece of fabric around the row of segments. Glue along the long edge.

6 From some card, cut out some eyes, fangs, and a tongue—you could decorate the eyes with glitter. Stick them to your snake. Give the body some stripes by sticking on some colorful ribbon. Poisonous animals are often brightly colored.

7 When your scary snake is finished, make a warning label to show people how dangerous it is.

Name: Subtractor
Size: Very long
Poisonous: Yes
Eats: Mice, birds, chips, and grown-ups
Habitat: Long grass and trees
Home: Hollow tree stumps and holes in the ground

Glossary

adapted
Animals that have changed over many generations to suit their living conditions.

altitude
The altitude of a place is its height above sea level.

Amazon basin
The part of South America drained by the Amazon River.

amphibian
An animal that can live both on land and in water, such as frogs, toads, newts, and salamanders.

anaconda
A large snake that kills prey animals by crushing them with their body.

Antarctica
The huge, cold continent around the South Pole. It is twice the size of Australia.

bladder
An organ found in the bodies of humans and animals. It stores urine, which is produced by the kidneys.

carrion
Dead or decaying flesh.

cocoon
A thin covering that some creatures make to enclose and protect themselves when they are not active.

crayfish
A lobster-like, freshwater creature.

decibels
A decibel is a unit used to measure the power of sound. The higher the decibel number, the louder the sound.

diabetes
A disease. People with untreated diabetes are unable to control the amount of glucose (a type of sugar) in their blood, and can feel very ill. Diabetes can be controlled with medicines, such as insulin.

dinosaur
A type of reptile that became extinct a very long time ago. One of the best known was *Tyrannosaurus rex*.

dry season
In tropical climates there can be dry and wet seasons. During the wet season rain falls heavily; during the dry season little or no rain falls.

extinct
If a species is extinct, it has died out—none of its kind are living.

fungi
Plants without leaves or flowers, such as mushrooms and toadstools. They grow on other plants or decayed material.

gecko
A small reptile. Geckos have toe pads that can stick to smooth surfaces. Some people keep geckos as pets.

gills
The organs that help animals that live in water to breathe. The gills take oxygen from the water.

larvae

A larva is the newly hatched form of many insects, before it has developed wings. Larvae change to become quite different-looking creatures as adults.

leaf litter

Dead plant material made from decaying leaves, twigs, and bark.

lure

Something such as an antenna, or strange-shaped tail, which looks like an insect or a worm. It is used by predators to attract creatures that will want to eat the lure, so that they instead may be caught.

mammal

Any warm-blooded animal with a backbone and hair. Mammals produce live young, not eggs. There are around 5400 species of mammal, ranging from the huge blue whale to the tiny bumblebee bat.

migrate

When animals migrate, they move from one place to another, usually as the seasons change and food becomes scarce.

native

The place where a creature, plant, or person originally comes from or was born.

predator

A creature that hunts and kills other animals for food.

rodent

A group of animals that includes mice, voles, squirrels, and shrews.

saliva

The liquid produced in the mouth to keep it wet and healthy.

secrete

To release liquid, especially from glands in the body.

species

A group of animals with similar characteristics to each other, and that can breed with each other.

tadpole

The newly hatched young of creatures such as frogs, toads, and newts.

tapir

A creature with a heavy body and short legs, similar in shape to a pig. It is related to the horse and the rhinoceros.

"third eye"

An organ that detects, or senses, light, found on the head of some reptiles.

toxin

A poisonous substance, especially one that is produced by bacteria. The saliva produced by the Komodo dragon is a toxin.

T-rex

T-rex is short for *Tyrannosaurus rex*—probably the most famous of the large, meat-eating dinosaurs.

tropical

Tropical relates to the tropics—the area on either side of the equator. The tropics are usually hot and damp.

venomous

A venomous creature uses poison, or venom, to paralyze or kill its prey.

wetlands

Naturally wet areas, such as marshes or swamps. They have spongy soil.

Index